NATIONAL GEOGRAPHIC



# People Live Here

George Wong

This is a desert.

People live here.

This is a plain.

People live here.

This is a mountain.

# People live here.

HANDLEBARS
FOOD & SALOON

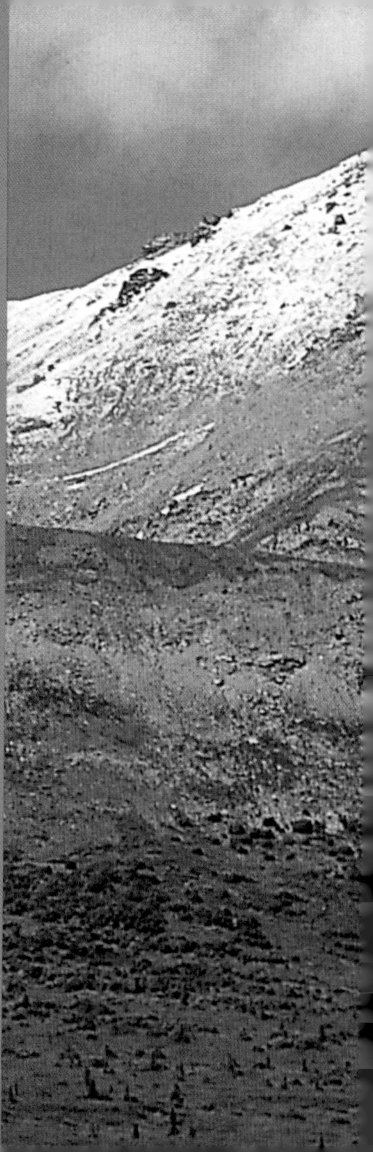

This is a forest.

People live here.

This is a wetland.

People live here.

This is a river.

# People live here.